The Rain Comes Again

by Sammy Playdon

First published 2024

© 2024 Springmead Publishing

ISBN: 978-1-9997082-6-9

For licensing requests, please contact the publisher at admin@springmead.org

Printed and bound in the UK
Images sourced from Freepik Premium

The Rain Comes Again

The rain comes again, time after time.
Without shelter we become drenched,
our clothes soaked through in water,
Oh how we complain and moan Lord.
We run away!
Hiding from the very vital substance you created for us to help
maintain life.
Showers of water that replenish the land
For which seeds take root to grow,
as to feed your animals of all species.
How strange we dislike getting rained upon.
Look Up!
Let this blessing from you Lord,
fall on our faces as a reminder of your greatness and spirit.
And as the vapour filled clouds gather,
and drops of rain start to fall,
let them nourish the roots of our souls,
as the forests and woodlands draw in
the nourishment for their roots.
The necessity of rain for dry,
drought ridden streams and rivers,
replenishes the homes for gill bearing animals to thrive in again.
Let us embrace the rains to come,
For we know whence they came from
And be Deeply Rooted in Christ

For further reading try these scriptures:
Jeremiah 9:21; Genesis 3:21; Job 37:10;
1 John 3:3; Jude 13; Psalm 86:5

People sitting on a palace roof.

People sitting on a palace roof,
Looking up to the night sky, clothed in sables and furs,
Seeing stars above their eyes,
And what are the names of the creatures, why do they live
and why are they scared?
It was dark and it was winter, with snow in the air,
dampness on their skin.
Satan arrives trying to steal their souls,
These tormented souls who were they
and where did there confusion come from?
They knelt, closed their eyes and prayed.
Then a fever of life bursts open,
Realising that from high, their lives meant something,
That his pure beautiful soul had ascended for their sins.
Lord we would dive into a freezing lake,
If we could for just one time, one time,
LOVE SOMEBODY THE WAY THAT YOU LOVE US

For further reading try these scriptures:
Psalm 68:4 & 8; Psalm 147:8; Psalm 148:4;
Acts 14:17; Hebrews 6:7; Hosea 10:12;
Joel 2:23-24; Job 5:10 & 36:27-29 & 37:6-16.

As the fine white clouds scatter and part

As the fine white clouds scatter and part,
The brilliant sunlight glowing through them,
Rays of light disperse and beam down on their creation.
Oh how the multicoloured pansies turn their faces
towards the sun,
Smiling as they dance amongst the gentle breeze,
They calmly nod their heads in praise and worship
to their creator.
The soil is rich and fertile
And with the whispering breath of God
Disperse their seeds increasing them in number.
How glorious creation everywhere.
From the delicate flowers to the sturdy robust trees.
Everything on earth comes from you and back to you Lord.
Sustaining us, in us around us, through all creation.
Mornings of our lives and there you are,
Bringing us our day in colour,
The sun between us,
We must reach out to you for gratitude and thanks
Our Lord of Lords
King of Kings

For further reading try these scriptures:
Psalm 103:15; Psalm 96:12; Psalm 72:19;
Ephesians 5:20; 1 Kings 4:33.

He sits under a lifeless brittle oak tree.

He sits under a lifeless brittle oak tree,
Barren, bare no leaves no shelter,
Why this confusion?
Oh his soul, he asks why do you ache so?
He sees a stream teaming with life abundantly,
Yet where am I ?
The stones are jagged beneath his feet,
These stones lead beyond the valley, the
path is the only way to the stream.
He must reach the water to survive.
He is desolate, lost, alone, a man
without purpose,
A man with an arid dry heart,
Trapped in himself,
He must continue ahead, he frets,
and is disillusioned to how he
became here.
Does anyone hear him or feel his pain? No one
cares.
His existence is a mere shell, the core of
his body rotten.
Clouds rapidly appear, blending together as mighty winds
stir up,

The rain begins to fall,

He looks up and cry's out,

Lord I can't see you, I need you, I can't find you.

The gusts become stronger,

He can't see, the rain affecting his vision,

He shouts louder and louder,

Help me Lord!

I repent, I repent

I'm lost in myself, the path ahead is one of destruction,

Oh mighty God

Save me from myself.

Immediately, the tangled knot of his

heart begins to unravel,

Healing to fullness and comfort from

his loving Father in Heaven.

My child, we rejoice in your plea for

help from us,

Never will we leave your soul and being.

This we vow we make to you Today.

Your Ever-Loving Father In Heaven

For further reading try these scriptures:
Psalm 31:21-24; Psalm 107:4-9;
Matthew 21:19.22; 2 Peter 1:8

Our Almighty Father God

Our Almighty Father God,
You are the beacon of all creation,
We give immense praise thanks and glory to your name,
for the very air we breathe,
and the voices you have given to us.
And it is with this gift of speech,
which only you Lord could have granted us,
we will amplify your name.
We thank you Lord.

From as far as the eyes can see
and beyond to the sun moon and stars,
your universal love for all creation.
The eternal coverage of love
that cushions our hearts with feathers of angels wings.
We thank you Lord.

The warmth and embrace from your brightly shining
beacon of light that
extends into heaven and on to us daily.
Minute by minute, hour by hour, week by week.
With hands of hope and harvest we praise your name Lord.
With feet of faith we will follow you Lord.

May we be wise to your teachings Lord and teach them well,
May that beacon that beats inside our hearts Lord,
be as beautiful in our motives as in our actions.
And just as the crest of a wave peaks and breaks
so you are there with every rise and fall.
We praise you Lord.

The core of this planet is a beacon too,
Lord life was designed and created by you,
Your beacons of light are a vastness even in the darkness
and stillness of night, they are there.
We praise you Lord.

A beacon of forgiveness you are Lord for all of our sins
each and every one of us,
Like the coral reefs beneath the expanse of the oceans,
You absorb them all.
We give thanks to you Lord.

We glorify and praise your name Lord
In the name of God The Father, God The Son & The Holy Spirit.

AMEN

For further reading try these scriptures:
Psalm 19:14 l; Job 33:3

I am your God!

I am your God!
My people which I have created,
With intelligence, reasoning and the ability to learn.
You have studied, watched and looked at nature,
From pondering minds, To adapt and be creative,
Mankind you have learnt how to travel on the vast oceans,
You have observed the insects travelling down streams on fallen
branches and leaves,
And created vessels to aid you to explore the waters, rivers and seas

FOR GOOD NOT DESTROY
You have observed the fowl of the air,
Their flight,
And in their motion,
Pondered,
And designed transport for flight,
FOR THE GOOD OF HUMANITY NOT DESTRUCTION

You have observed all creatures,
Building their homes,
From the debris of trees,
Sheddings of animal hair,
To build homes for yourselves
FOR THE GOOD OF HUMANITY TO SHARE AND NOT SELFISHNESS

You have observed the mountains,
And there the minerals and irons they house,
And mined them for trade, benefits and money,
FOR THE GOOD OF HUMANITY TO BE SHARED NOT GREED AND
PRIDE

You have observed the seeds, plants, and trees,
Harvested them,
To feed and nourish one another,
FOR GOOD TO BE SHARED, NOT SELFISHNESS

You have observed the oceans
And the marine life,
For a source of food and nourishment,
FOR GOOD NOT FOR DESTRUCTION AND POLLUTION

I created Man and woman!
To multiply,
All to be unique!
TO DO GOOD NOT TO DEFAME AND KILL

Here is the complete difference my children,
Of my creation and love for humanity,
Before the fall,
And Satan's hatred for love and kindness is clear !

I urge you all!
Examine your hearts and souls and minds,
To do what is MY WILL
To know which is good and lovely,

Against Satan's chaos and lies

AMEN

For further reading try these scriptures:
Hebrews 13:16; 1 Timothy 6:17-19;
James 3:7; Psalm 73:6;
Proverbs 1:18-19, Proverbs 13:10-11.

Our children who are on earth

Our children who are on earth,
Blessed are those whom believe, for we are with you,
For from us you receive your daily needs.
My son Jesus was sent to heal and save,
For those who can't see,
As Satan plots and schemes, trying to steal your identities,
We pray for their hearts,
To be lifted and free!
You see us in the stars, the universe and sea.
For it is written!
The word was spoken for all to adhere to.
Share this my Children!
Pray for those that no not from whence they came.
For the time is nigh for our book to close,
Brothers and Sisters united to save,
With us you will be in eternity!
This is our Promise to all whom see,

That my Son Jesus Christ is the saviour and IS
The only way to Me!
The glory my children you will find,
As we light the way,
Your Mighty Trinity!
The earth is ours and ours alone!
Material things don't mean much and of no use to us!
It's your hearts we desire, and for you to know us and seek.
Your rewards in Heaven will be peace, health and harmony,
Your spirits free.
Our children stay focused and pray with us, as the closing stages commence,
Only, Only in Your God You Must Trust!
Satan will try and deceive with lies, telling you you're not worth much,

His nest of vipers, biting at
your heels!!!
When he senses you are lost
and want to give up,
remember he is the betrayer
of life!
His evil army won't come to
much!!
So when he strikes be
READY and PRAY!
Kneel down to us, for it
is us the TRINITY who
will save.
The battle was won on the
day life began.
We are creators of thee,
In us have faith and
believe.
Swim away from the dead
wood and murky depths,
living without purpose,
Your worth is in creation
itself!
For this earth we designed
for you my children
for you to dwell!
Our angels will sing and
rejoice with thine hearts,

The trumpets will sound
above the clouds,
Roars of thunder heard upon
the ground,
Hearts beating like drums,
For the broken to be found.
Do not tarry!
We repeat,
The time is near!
Repent for your sins, and let
your hearts be healed.
Freely we love you ALL and
freely we give to ALL
Oh, people of GOD,
Shout out in praise,
receive us today!
Above all be like
finely tuned
harps,
Instruments of God,
Be ready and Pray,
In every circumstance! In
our names
Worship, Pray and Love
each other,
Until the, The End !!
For My Children whom we
Adore.

For further reading try these scriptures:
Psalm 82:6, Psalm 127:3; Psalm 37:7 & 12;
Proverbs 23:32; Proverbs 24:8;
2 Thessalonians 2:7-16; 2 Thessalonians 3:1-5.

Highlight The Sounds That We Hear

Highlight the sounds that we hear Lord. Are we listening?
Oh the revelation of sound is a conduit of creation. Lord our God
Let us be mindful of everything we hear.
The sounds of footsteps when we walk on different surfaces Listen!
In silence and quiet times are we hearing the beauty and tranquillity of that?
Are we listening to the various echoes of sound Lord?
Powerful gusts of winds swirling through the leaves, to the rustle of a breeze lifting them gently

Are we listening Lord?
Different directions of gales whistling sounds we hear in open meadows and fields. Listen!
The drip drop of water landing on various surfaces, slow paced droplets of water, torrential rains pelting against window panes.
The crackling, smouldering embers in a fire, the sizzling and spitting of produce cooking, the blaze of a wild fire scorching the valleys and plains. Listen!
Oh what different sounds akin to musical instruments,

Are we listening Lord?
Communication of your animal kingdom Lord
Every species can communicate with one another. Listen!
Languages speech, conversations, laughter, joy, singing, awareness of someone's cry, pain, sorrow, hurt, injury.
Are we listening Lord? We have become deaf!

Too busy to listen and hear the sounds of life that is alive,
which you spoke into creation!!
Absorb the sounds around us.

As humans we become distant from you Lord!
Thinking you are silent and not talking to us. Listen!!
Be mindful of this ability to hear.
Not only can we hear one sound at any moment Lord.
You so intricately designed us to hear sophisticated sounds all
at once in unison, to remind us whatever time day or night
hearing is boundless, high low, wherever one turns, in every
place, completely, at all points of the universe.
Let us not take this sense to hear for granted!
The Lords spirit is pouring out and available to humanity.
Observe this and be full of his spirit that flows through
everything!
ARE WE REALLY LISTENING?

Lord, we thank you wholeheartedly for the sense of hearing,
In awe we are of this ability you have granted us.
We Will Praise Honour and Worship you!!
Oh Mighty God Our Creator

AMEN

For further reading try these scriptures:
Psalm 42:7-8; Psalm 94:8-9; Job 12:7-11;
Isaiah 1:2; Isaiah 34:1; Isaiah 50:4-5;
Hebrews 5:11; John 8:43; Acts 13:16;
1 Corinthians 2:10; Matthew 10:27; Matthew 11:15

If Only

Tainted, tormented, twisted beings everywhere,
Lost in treasures they desire,
Dying inside, despite the hordes of things they buy!
If only I had this, If only I had that,
Maybe if I was famous and well known,
Maybe if I was taller or even shorter,
If only I was someone else and had someone else's life.
Everyone else seems happier than me,
How can that be?
Life is not fair you see.
So, the despair I hide is kept inside,
The mask I wear, keeps you from knowing the real me!
For all these things I now know to be untrue,
For that moment of prayer Heaven touched my being,
And released my soul from the chains and bondage,
That had me captive for all my days.
Praise and honour, Lord Jesus
The saviour of our souls, To the ends of the earth,
I will bow down to you Lord,
Forever I will follow you,
Forever I will be grateful and thankful,
For the mercy you have given me.

For further reading try these scriptures:
Proverbs 2719-21
Psalm 27: 1-4
James 5:3